GATHERING

THE

WINDS

Also by Pina Pipino

The Scent of Time (2014)
Whispers and Voices (2011)

Flight of Doves (Chapbook, 1999)
No One Knows His Name (Chapbook, 1995)
There Were Other Willows (Chapbook, 1992)

GATHERING

THE

WINDS

New Poems
By

Pina Pipino

L' Orange Press
Bloomfield, New Jersey
USA

Library of Congress Control Number: 2018911065
Gathering the Winds/ Pina Pipino
Poems
First Edition
ISBN: 978-0-578-20758-2

L' Orange Press
Bloomfield, New Jersey, USA
lorangepresspub@gmail.com

Front & back covers and book design by Karen Hubbard
Front cover painting: "Autumnal Wind" by Harunobu Suzuki

ACKNOWLEDGEMENT

I am indebted to Sharon Spencer, professor of Creative Writing at Montclair State University, who first believed in and encouraged my attempts at writing.

I am very thankful to Grace Cunningham, Georgiana Hart, Karen Hubbard, Norma Miller, Maggie Mohr, Phillipa Scott, Maryann Siebert, Peggy Vasallo and Nina Ziv for their help and support with this collection.

For Eduardo, Graciela,
Cailla, Lindsay, Alex, Danielle and
Raelan Skye

Better be a swan, or a crane … riding the winds
High up, well known to the clouds where they fly.

Han Shan (8th c.)

TABLE OF CONTENTS

TITLE

Tonight I Can Write

The night is starry
and the stars are blue and shiver in the distance.
The night wind revolves in the sky and sings.

Pablo Neruda   (1904-1973)

SOMETIMES

Sometimes   I would like to gather the cold winds
     in my hands and warm them   then let go
     so there will be endless warmth

sometimes   I whisper a wish that nobody hears
     close my eyes and see the wish come true–
     it doesn't matter if it's just make believe

sometimes   on a windy night   I gaze upwards
     and watch the stars   watch me
     but   not even one answers

sometimes   the moon visits the pond   a quiet wind echoes in
                                                    the valley
     it wanders like a listless cloud
     unsettles the waters

sometimes   when the wind takes me to a dreamlike space
     I hear Angelus bells tell each other
     those ancient tales

sometimes   I forget that life is a succession of fleeting moments
     sown together
     in a quilt of uneven memories.

An English Breeze

Forth and to travel with the breeze
While, swift and singing, smooth and strong
She gallops by the fields along.

Robert Louis Stevenson   (1850-1894)

ILLUSIONS

At times   I feel I know you and trust settles
   it is then I learn   I must give time a chance
   to show me what you really are

At times   I see that hawk daily circling in my sky
   as if nothing but gliding were in his mind
   until he darts down and catches a vole

At times   I feel an urge
   to dance   and run   and jump as I did
   then my body sighs and smiles   remembering

At times   I close my eyes   and spring wings   and fly
   to the five-thousand-mile-long Great Wall of China
   along with one-thousand origami cranes

At times   I go round and round in circles   believing
   "Whatever I clearly and distinctly perceive is true"
   then Descartes adds "Senses sometimes deceive us"

At times   I'm sure even the smallest piece in the puzzle
   found its place in my universe
   try not to miss the lost piece

At times   the sky is so close   and so bright
   it overrides the blueness inside
   and I lose track of the horizon

At times   there is an echo of memories   and I feel
   the truth of the past   as the stars shimmer
   in the river   and a wish stains the waters.

A Sunset

These vapors, with their leaden, golden, iron, bronzed glows,
Where the hurricane, the waterspout, thunder, and hell repose,
Muttering hoarse dreams of destined harms.

Victor Hugo   (1802-1885)

MOTHERS

I am the daughter of white spiders hidden
    between pages
    pages housed behind glass at the home library

I am the daughter of the Zonda wind blowing
    blowing
    amid sugarcane plantations and orange groves

I am the daughter of the Evening Star that lost its light
    but at the end of the universe
    I found my own light in a black hole

I am the daughter of the Train to the Clouds that stopped
    stopped at mid-bridge but I left it standing
    and turned back to find my own path

I am the daughter nursed on sweetened opium-tea
    tea brewed from red poppies growing in the garden
    when I woke up I began dreaming

I am the daughter of dark ink polluting the creek
    dead grasshoppers floating like dried flesh
    torn from Methuselah

I am the daughter of the olive-green sierras that dissolved
    in the endless night
    and searches for light inside the stars

I am the daughter who survived the assassin's knife
    though I do not remember how
    nor know why

I am the daughter who prayed at the altar of Mary
    when candles were unlit
    curlicue mosaic floors blurred in the fog

I am the daughter of the Toba tribe
    who roams the Zodiac
    but is outcast

I am the daughter of indifference
    masked as love
    that slides like muck

I am the daughter searching for his pauper's grave   carved out
    of the Tupungato and when someone crawls inside
    phosphorescent bones illuminate the walls

I am the daughter of "E lucevan le stele"
    sang while laundering at the tub
    but nobody sings

I am the daughter of a stone thrower   stones thrown
    thrown before black nimbuses covered the house
    thrown before the storm knocked down the walls

I am the daughter born first   to live with strange strangers
    who spoke with forked tongues
    and wore hurtful words engraved on their foreheads

I am the daughter swaddled in air
    fed wild berries on moonless nights
    clothed with strawberries embroidered on white cotton

I am the daughter of a long lost tale of pain   assuaged with
    scented balms but when butterflies alighted on the dressing
    the wounds still bled

I am the daughter who ate stir fried sparrows
   unable to hatch
   on newly made nests

I am the daughter who knows everything and nothing
I am   the daughter.

The Heart Has Narrow Banks

Till Hurricane bisect
And as itself discerns
Its insufficient Area
The heart convulsive learns.

       Emily Dickinson   (1830-1886)

FATHERS

We   loved as only children can   unconditionally
        absorbed the ancient ways of a foreign land, imagined
        life at the top of the Italian Alps, where nobody lives

we   loved life on the farm   with spaces to hide
        watered the vegetable garden, weeded the spider-laden
        rose garden learned adults are a mystery   and conditioning

we   sucked sweetness from sugarcane   always sweet
        drank droplets of kindness
        feared tropical storms   alone

we   played like children   who knew better
        had friends in our dogs   they loved us
        but we were not us   we were shadows in the dark

we   loved the sky when it was not black
        heard deafening silences
        were sleeping when the roof caved in

we   felt the emptiness of his absence
        we   carry all
        inside.

The Growth of Love

And bitter northwinds then withheld the spring,
That dallied with her promise till 'twas lost.

Robert Seymour Bridges   (1844-1930)

DEATH

True   the black carriage was pulled by two lustrous black horses
tears fell onto what might have been
life felt like yesterday's wearisome walk

True   he was in the coffin as if he weren't there
bereft of flowers other than a few
like the interlude in a garden started

True   sitting on a chair as stark as dead stars   afar
I felt there was no roof over my head
ghostly shadows flew up to the cosmic vault

True   with eyes closed I saw fragments of kind words left
on the ground, traces of unheeded promises made under
tropical suns, awed of his stories wrapped in Old
                                   Filaments

True   gone are the celery salads we had under the apricot trees
the sweaty smell of smoke from the locomotive fire
all lost in the ceaseless winds swirling in sidereal spaces

True   I stepped on the Camino viale, before the ancestral house
I pictured him and his father leaning on the verandah
there was the angst of things lost in the fissures of time

True   his grave is in a faraway land   with a lock on the past
a past that filters a story interrupted
a slender thread of lost wishes and desires

True   my arms feel the need to hug him   as if he cared
need to hear his voice no matter in what language
need to rest my head on his knees and hear the tales.

I Meant to Find Her When I Came

To wander—now--is my Repose--
To rest—To rest would be
A privilege of Hurricane
To Memory—and Me.

Emily Dickinson   (1830-1886)

DECEIT

Smiles curled like a tiger's tail
    colorful tales told at the edge of time
    where embers resembled the warmth of the heart

Smiles on our lips   daggers in her eyes
    infancy believed the illusion   childhood saw the illusion
    the last grain of sand in the hourglass sighed

Smiles and the taste of clover-honey poured into the cochlea
    illusions were resilient   nothing else was there
    the skies were grey wherever we went

Smiles   wine   a smiling moon   a surreal reality invited
    the senses surrendered   the mind didn't mind
    truth slid helplessly into the smooth folds of deceit

Smiles untied the knot that kept doors closed
    there was no indication that the potential may not be
    I forgot that evil is one of the elements

Smiles of the surreptitious kind reach back in time
    remember where and when they learned
    that there is always one more draught to sate

Smiles with promises blowing in the wind
    a hand comes near
    there is always a reliable emptiness

Smiles hued like flames rise to the sky
    inflamed primeval malice
    unseen winds of artifice feed them.

Wind On The Hill

So then I could tell them
Where the wind goes....
But where the wind comes from
Nobody knows.

Alan Alexander Milne   (1882-1956)

IMPOTENCE

I saw it wander above lakes   seas   oceans   earth
   and not once acknowledge I was there

I saw the snow covered Aconcagua, whiteness melt under the sun
   it was not easy to walk under a white veil

I saw it come and go through the aspen copes
   as birds flew into the teeth of the wind

I saw it at the hour of the ox   beat   bleed   drip
   as if it were the only organ in my carcass

I saw a river of ink slide on the blank page
   words washed out with the tide

I saw fireflies in a jar   lights out   eyes closed   inert
   but alive

I saw a cricket crying outside   tears fell to the lawn
   with each jump

I saw the shadow   of white geese flying north
   losing themselves in the cold

I saw it on the porch as the earth was pelted with tropical rain
   scented vapors rising with the summer heat

I saw all of these   awake at the hour of the ox.

The Time Before

Their day was ringing the barrens in a loud wind
and they were taking their seasons with them as animals
through the beating light urging on the sheep of autumn.

W.S.Merwin   (1927-   )

SILENCIO

Quiet on the wet sand   all bodies lie inert
    wave by wave bathe
    seeds sown on hope

Quiet in the soul   as sunlight is chased by moonlight
    as the wind sings its longing
    as Diotima whispers her ancient wisdom

Quiet in the forest as the Langur nurses her young
    as each tree remembers the Great Remembering
    as the owl discerns his own dreams

Quiet in Utopia as Pantagruel wails
    hush in the night as Minos evaluates my fate
    and celestial bodies move without being moved

Quiet in the old house that breathes its pestilent breath
    that sees the lies in the face of liars
    that lets nocturnal shadows roam free

Quiet on the alfalfa fields of childhood
    on the long road lined with palos borrachos
    on the long dirt path muddied by rain

Quiet on the distant cerro San Pedro
    on the Ascension procession
    on the convent's patio weighed with echoes of laughter.

Walt Whitman

O swift wind! O space and time!
Now I see it is true what I guessed at
I am afoot with my vision.

Walt Whitman   (1819-1892)

POSSESSIONS

I have one heart to last me to the end of life
    each beat a stroke of luck
    emanating from the unknown

I have memories sneak up on me when I sense
    a companion   an unwanted companion
    that comes from the shadows of time

I have a bundle of love that echoes throughout the cosmos
    wends round distant stars
    visits incipient galaxies

I have inside   a place of deep silence
    where I curl up and dream
    like a somnolent mimosa

I have heard the aspen's leaves tremble with wishes from before
    when life began   illusions were strong
    and I knew they all would come true

I have secret thoughts locked inside Hypanthia's ellipse
    a well-known dwelling of changing seasons
    inescapable bouts of joy and woe

I have longed for the brightness of dawn to come
    when the darkness of night was unending
    when the eyes stayed open   searching

I have taken my tale to the river   for the waters listen
    gather my story and cleanse it
    wrap it in waves of forgiveness

I have entered the temple of silent ghosts awaiting
    the promised expiation of time
    that may never come

I have turned and seen a rainbow touch my shadow
    I smiled at the eternal truth
    that I'm just a cloud passing through.

The Breeze at Dawn

The breeze at dawn has secrets to tell you.
Don't go back to sleep.

Jelaludin Rumi   (1207-1273)

GHOSTS

The wind groaned above the stormy tropical vastness
    I was a shadow
    I breathed alone   like a solitary bird hidden in its nest
    next to the edge of that ageless dirt lane

The wind rushed in with ferocity to rough up the uppermost top
    of fig trees that grew by the flustered stream
    I was a shadow
    thirsty for the time that was a dream time

The wind defied the red crowned cranes that struggled west
    after the darting steam locomotive
    I was a shadow
    heard her insults rise above the train's persistent percussion

The wind pushed heavy rain against the window panes
    there was no moon swimming at the bottom of the well
    I was a shadow
    there and not there   trembling

The wind filtered through the slits in window frames
    through the sliver of spaces between doors and floors
    I was a shadow
    watched bricks loosened, falling from those walls of long ago

The wind ran on grooves of line after line of red Spanish tiles
    where bulbous black spiders huddled in their thick white webs
    I was a shadow
    prayed one of them wouldn't fall and nest on my blond mane

The wind whistled like violins weeping between seasons
    I was a shadow
    heard staccato violas scare swallows huddled in the rafters
    I was a shadow....

The Gypsy and the Wind

And while she tells them, weeping,
Of her strange adventure
The wind furiously gnashes
Against the slate roof tiles.

Federico Garcia Lorca   (1898-1936)

THREAD OF TALES

I found the thread that ties me to the beginning
   of time when there was only a hint
   of soil floating on a sea of untold turmoil

I found the thread that hangs from clouds of sulfur
   clouds that roamed
   before there were suns

I found the thread that binds me to infinite spaces
   with mists billowing in the eternal muddle
   of being   longing   knowing and not knowing

I found the thread that sang without sounds
   but no one cared for there was no one there
   to gather the thread of song

I found the thread that fell from the end of the universe
   whirled amid gasses and minerals and enzymes
   after eons of waiting   waiting   waiting

I found the thread that twirled around me
   when I wasn't yet me   but I was there
   wanting   wanting   wanting

I found the thread of violins speaking the truth
   the truth that no one wants to hear
   but they all hear its musical wails

I found the thread that binds me to Earth
   earth that has me here
   though it didn't want me.

Come, Come Thou Bleak December Wind

Come, come thou bleak December wind,
And blow the dry leaves from the tree!

Samuel Taylor Coleridge   (1772-1834)

REGRETS

I wish I never wrote that letter as if it were mine
    every word dictated by her rage
    as he read   he bent under the weight of his life
    like an aging cherry tree devoid of leaves

I wish I had remembered   or someone
    had reminded me
    it was my brother's birthday
    the day of my wedding

I wish I had been a rebel
    had not flinched at punishment
    had not hidden behind my shadow
    had followed my soul when it ran

I wish the fog that clouded me
    had dissipated somewhat
    let me see who I was
    let me be.

That Wind I Used To Hear It Swelling

That Wind I used to hear it swelling
With joy divinely deep
You might have seen my hot tears welling
But rapture made me weep.

Emily Jane Bronte   (1818-1848)

ETUDE

Maybe firs in the forest have secrets
   they share with the wind
   before rain washes them away

Maybe the ocean splashes the rocks
   to sing a song without pause
   to souls sitting and thirsting at the shore

Maybe the woes of weeping willows
   are whispered in between soft drizzles
   because hope lingers

Maybe fog is the sadness of the sea
   longing for a bright morning   and
   the smell of chestnuts roasting on the hearth

Maybe dreams are shadows of something real
   born beyond time and space
   like undying memories brought by the wind.

The Wind

Each wave flings up a shower of pearls,
Laughing, dancing, sunny wind,
Whistling, howling, rainy wind.

Amy Lowell   (1874-1925)

EDGES

At the edge of that musical lament quivering in the quena
    resonates the echo of an Inca's angst

At the edge of the harvest moon's aura   lingers a plea
    as raw as the smell of autumn's burnt leaves

At the edge of the backyard where the old weeping willow weeps
    there is a buried secret that seeps into its core

At the edge of the dream that fades like a nebula
    there is an image of the unimaginable

At the edge of the Delphi oracle   Socrates whispers
    "Poets write poetry by a sort of wisdom and imagination"

At the edge of awareness   the self hesitates
    between what it is and what it longs to be

At the edge of a life without a past   the future beckons
    there is no way to escape the call of the heavens

At the edge of the other side of the world
    I remembered those things that never happened

At the edge of a pebble garden there is a marble sculpture
    and everything harmonizes like a perfect chord

At the edge of the Yellow sea, Mazu helps paper boats
    glide into the world of dreams

At the edge of the Ionian sea   Miletus tells us
    "Nothing is stronger than necessity"

At the edge of a forest   we see each tree has its own shape
    just as I can only be what I am.

To The Man-of-War-Bird

Thou born to match the gale
To cope with heaven and earth and sea and hurricane,
Thou ship of air that never furl'st thy sails.

Walt Whitman (1819-1892)

ACHE

To suffer disappointment was emptiness of what was promised
    of what was wanted   of what was expected
    promises withering on the road I treaded

To suffer seemed to be part of the deal of living
    a deal I didn't agree to or sign to live by
    to see flowers bloom in spring or blood drenching battlefields

To suffer was in the wails of a babe   at night
    when she could not sleep as soundly
    as when she bobbed inside the womb

To suffer in the bones was felt later in the walk
    when knees were replaced   when the spine ached
    and groaned   asking for a rest

To suffer was not what I wanted   it was what I got
    what I graduated from
    wounds are invisible diplomas hanging on the inner wall

To suffer permeates life in the entire kingdom
    as when spiders are crushed under my shoe
    or when the eagle sinks her talons into a baby muskrat

To suffer is the unwelcome load I carry on my shoulders
    one which at times is so light   it doesn't seem to be there
    at times it makes me gasp for air   and stumble

To suffer and to laugh can happen in unison
    as when I lost my job at Christmas time
    and nobody knew.

Leaving It to You

Catch the wind while you tether shadows.

    Kuan Hsiu   (832-912)

SOMEONE DOES

Some peer at infinite distances
    between light and darkness
    discern   hidden paths

Some see that everyone has a shadow
    which sometimes points the way
    sometimes walks behind

Some walk at the river's edge
    follow cherry petals speeding away on the stream
    count them fast   before they drown

Some listen to violin strains filter between aspen leaves
    leaves rustled by warm summer breezes
    and say hasty farewells

Some see waves roll from immense oceans
    with a heart full of things to say
    but   to whom

Some watch rain fall over ancient mountains
    as time washes away their trail
    and a steep cliff is obscured by haze

Some hear an evening bell chime
    where red suns set countless times
    over songs sung long ago.

The Wind One Brilliant Day

The wind, one brilliant day, called
To my Soul with an odor of jasmine.

Antonio Machado   (1875-1939)

EFFECT

If   I sleep soundly
   thoughts ignite in the morning

If   the way is difficult and long
   a warm wind takes me to the end

If   loneliness tangles or untangles in the air
   even the stars dim their eyes

If   water runs smoothly in the manse
   smiles defeat loss   lost in dust and sand.

The Wind

The wind is without there and howls in the trees

Robert Louis Stevenson   (1850-1894)

OVERSEER

It is here and on this summer it will see me
    sow seeds of fear on the swamp
    where they will drown

It is here and it will sweep the debris
    I do not see
    though it is there stenching illusions

It is here and it will record how wide the stars
    wend from each other
    and if they ever meet in secret spheres

It is here to remind me of parents
    who brought their young ones
    to watch the man hang from a noose

It is here to follow the trace of footprints dented
    into the snow   counting the road-kill left
    on the way to supremacy

It is here and it steps on the path that leads
    to the mountaintop to stop lava
    from drowning villagers in the valley

It is here and it dips its hands in the seven seas
    infested with oil spills
    gasses bubbling to the surface

It is here to count how many years
    between one war
    and another   other   other

It is here to help in the search for the other half
    of the world
    the half willing to extend a hand

It is here to tell me whether Love is indeed
    the eldest and noblest and mightiest
    of the gods.

The Growth of Love

To fortune's wind the sails of purpose spread.

Robert Seymour Bridges   (1844-1930)

DINNING

Dinner with twelve friends   an old olive tree stands vigilant
    like feathers carried by the breeze   the spaces whisper omens
    the room is full of shadows   wine and bread are blessed
    visions of Golgotha loom

Dinner on the terrace on tropical evenings   blue-black heavens
    filled with Southern stars   sometimes there was moonlight
    fragrance of jasmine   the sound of crickets on the lawn
    I longed for time to stop

Dinner inside on tropical winters, coal aglow on the brick stove
    handmade spinach-with-brain ravioli
    her calm at the table was fragile   the heart remembers things
    that often happened

Dinner at restaurants in Buenos Aires   on visiting days
    exquisite food we savored   we will not have it everyday
    echoes from the past   the illusion of unity
    one more wound

Dinner in Essex Fells   four minds folded onto themselves
    when the sun went down and night fell
    a tear darkened the world
    the season of blossoms had passed

Dinner with friends at embattled times   is a melody for the soul
    together we ponder Socrates' words
    "Hope is the only good that is common to all men".

Walt Whitman

The sound of the belch'd words of my voice, voice loos'd to the
                                                                eddies
Of the wind.

    Walt Whitman   (1819-1892)

IMMORTALS

Adam did not invent anything, did not create poetry or melodies
    did not leave behind lofty architecture   but was the first man
    to blame others for his folly   the first man whose penis
    languidly rests on his thigh   like a trusting babe waiting
    waiting on the glorious Sistine Chapel to come to life
    at the touch of the elder in the Trinity

Homer who no one knows where in Greece was born or when
    nor whether he is the only author of the Iliad and Odyssey
    he lives shrouded in the fog of time immemorial
    has inspired legions of poets with his songs
    about the manipulation of man by the gods
    of Achilles' weak spot, Ulysses' travails, Penelope's undoings

Confucius said "What you don't want done to yourself,
    don't do to others"; in the Spring and Autumn of his country.
    Spring of thought from a teacher for whom
    "Ignorance is the night of the mind, but a night without moon
    or stars"; in the Autumn of strife and descent of empire, he
    advised, "When you have faults do not fear to abandon them"

Michelangelo who was born in Caprece and made Tuscany
    the birth place of his David   that posed to strike a giant
    much like an ant against a praying mantis
    David pried from a block of pink marble that time tarnished
    to a mellow flesh tone that startles
    and who is now a star at the Academia

Cervantes who brought to life the dreamer of La Mancha
    the one who chased after windmills, like a lion
    at the heel of gazelles, proudly galloped on Rocinante
    a medieval knight who ran after imaginary giants
    an unhinged Fury who stared at starry nights dreaming of
    Dulcinea   ——   everything was true to his eyes

Shakespeare who did much ado about everyone and everything
    to our delight   amusement   horror   despair
    and asked of a skull THE question
    he who immersed us in the ultimate tempest
    rendered page after page of slaughtered kings and princes–
    we will forever weep for the assailed lovers we couldn't save.

The Rain and the Wind

Ever the rain—the rain and the wind!
Come, hunch with me over the fire,
Dream of the dreams that leered and grinned.

William Ernest Henley   (1849-1902)

IMAGINATION

Imagine a world where leaders ended countries differences
    with a handshake instead of the threat of a nuclear doom

Imagine the human body so perfect that it never gives birth
    to babies with birth defects

Imagine this planet so wholesome   it doesn't bury villages
    with mudslides   tornadoes   earthquakes   tsunamis

Imagine people so at peace with themselves and others
    newspapers exist only to print good deeds

Imagine a file of ducks skimming a quiet lake   deer in the forest
    and the National Rifle Association doesn't sell death

Imagine this planet as a community of different peoples
    who welcome one another with melodies   art   smiles

Imagine   just for a moment   imagine.

Who Has Seen the Wind?

Who has seen the wind?
Neither you nor I:
But when the trees bow down their heads,
The wind is passing by.

Christina Rossetti   (1830-1894)

ANDANTE MODERATO

There were mountains meant to link earth with the heavens
    dark clouds threatening the moon
    shadows wrapped in mystery
    messages whispered in the autumn breeze
    echoes fading in the night
    debts owed me   written in Father's soul
    old gods ignoring my prayers

There was the first sign marking a destiny
    a story being born
    a road I did not see
    a measure of sorrow
    a farewell that came too soon
    a boundless world so unfair
    that old willow with a stab in the trunk

There is new grass sprouting in spring
    a sorceress evoking dreams
    a share of joy and sadness
    a murmur of doves
    the healing of tears
    gold in the evening sky
    andante moderato in the stream.

Daffodils

I wander'd lonely as a cloud
That floats on high o'er vales and hills,
When all at once I saw a crowd,
A host, of golden daffodils;
Beside the lake, beneath the trees,
Fluttering and dancing in the breeze.

William Wordsworth   (1770-1850)

LOVE

Love spreads its wings   made of sighs and moans
    feathery wisps of appetite that arouse the beloved
    he is the ruler of pleasures and desires

Love summers at Agra amid alabaster
    lovers sense its essence in the temple to ache immortal
    that shuns dissemblers

Love is awake in the twilight dawn at Mount Elikonas
    in the Andes on cold winter nights
    in the Yanomami tribe under the Amazonia canopy

Love is never lonely   it stills harsh winds   sooths wounds
    doesn't let dark shadows close in   blows on dandelion seeds
    that climb to the clouds

Love endures time   it is a poet and the source of poetry
    when it touches us   we become poets
    words unravel like a thread of silk

Love illuminates a dark night as the Vespertine star does
    it doesn't let warfare invade the soul
    it lets the water go where it's meant to go

Love asks dragonflies to run ahead of approaching storms
    like ant explorers warning of dangerous paths
    then we see the long road to the sun

Love is the loyal friend that lives in me
    lets me see wings of angels in the air
    lets me touch the Milky Way on summer nights.

The Wind

O wind, a-blowing all day long,
O wind, that sings so loud a song!

Robert Louis Stevenson   (1850-1894)

POESIA

On a perfect moment   just before the first word is written
    Calliope enters the poet's mind
    stirs her blood
    traps her into her spell

on a stroll by the stream   there   where the water gathers
    under the canopy of acacias and turns towards the meadow
    the poet lounges on the grass   gazes at the waiting paper
    like a thirsty Bedouin in the desert

on a walk amid sequoia trees the poet imagines dinosaurs
    resting at the shade of these red giants
    huge bodies slumber afraid of nothing
    other than the infernal hurricanes   in her mind

on a dark day illumined by the thoughts of numberless fireflies
    alight on the walls   the poet closes her eyes
    and sees a red apple asleep in the basket on the kitchen table
    as if left there by Snow White after the bite

on a despairing moment after the fight   she slides into her shell
    silence envelops her   and she still slides
    until she reaches that deep silky nook
    in solitude   like a resentful mollusk

on a summer day the poet slices an orange
    in quarters   sinks her teeth into the juicy pulp
    juice drips down her neck
    sweetness reaches down   down

on a frightful insular night   the poet is lost in the woods
    leaves hiss above her like bats' wings speeding
    in a flash of light Virgil admonishes
    "Let thy words be clear"

on a day as placid as the smile on a child   the aroma
    of carnations in the garden   and mint near the pond
    spreads like vapors from the heavens
    makes her forget the fog.

To A Child Dancing In The Wind

Dance there upon the shore;
What need have you to care
For wind or water's roar?

William Butler Yeats   (1865-1939)

BEAUTY

Beauty is as fragile as sunrays filtering
    through the wispy silk of a kimono's sleeve

Beauty is as intense as the immaculate summit of Mount Fuji
    thrusting against the azure

Beauty is as purposeful as the lentissimo movements
    of Butoh dancers bathed in moonlight

Beauty is as silent as waves folding onto themselves
    on placid nights

Beauty is as strident as fireworks exploding
    in unison

Beauty is as iridescent as the radiant surface
    of a mother of pearl.

Blow, Blow, Thou Winter Wind

Blow, blow, thou winter wind
Thou are not so unkind
As a man's ingratitude;
Thy tooth is not so keen,
Because thou are not seen,
Although thy breath be rude.

William Shakespeare   (1564-1616)

LIKE THAT

Like herons migrate in unison
    to sing their song up north

Like a river flows in the valley
    to dwell in the ocean swell

Like cherry-tree blooms tumble on the lawn
    then are no more

Like shooting stars that disappear in the expanse
    are not seen twice

Like salmon swim against northern flows
    until death overcomes them

Like a mimulus flower folds for life
    at a mere touch

Like a drove of doves scatters
    at the sound of a shot

Like the overwhelmed heart
    stops

So I want the memory of your face
    to be gone.

The Waste Land

The wind
Crosses the brown land, unheard.

       T.S. Eliot   (1888-1965)

SOLITUDE

Regard one day waiting for the next
    like a string of wishes
    threaded with a sigh

Regard that sparrow poised on the low branch
    see her drift toward l'amour
    wings swallowed by desired dusk

Regard the story in search of a storyteller
    telling a tale as brief as a butterfly's gasp
    as elusive as fireflies escaped from the jar

Regard the moon waning at the edge of that cloud
    she knows
    too much light makes secrets die

Regard spring still hesitant   still unsure
    everything feels so fragile
    like the first leaves on awakening oaks

Regard what happens today
    as part of my tomorrow
    a landscape of lost dreams.

Why Moan, Why Wail You, Wind of Night

Why moan, why wail you, wind of night,
With such despair, such frenzied madness?

Fyodor Ivanovich Tyutchev (1803-1873)

LOST AND FOUND

I lost sight of cherry blooms smiling to the sun
saw a windfall of petals spread on the lawn
boughs without nascent green buds
    I found the annual promise of rebirth in the sight and song
    of Warblers   Red-eyed Vireos   Robins

I lost my way in the land of shadows
where everyone was a shadow
a singsong told me not to flounder
    I found my way out through the fog
    candlelight flickered on the walls   I was home

I lost my way back into that dream
I knew that dreams are the umbra of something real
and some dreams bury the image of the unimaginable
    I found that hope is a ribbon of stars tied round the world
    resigned myself that what was in that dream   was not mine

I lost the strength to delve deeper into the darkness
even though Socrates told me that
"The most difficult thing in life is to know yourself"
    I found many truths thrown at me in life
    with Goethe I realized that "You at the end are what you are"

I lost the path that leads to the paradise we all long for
wandered at night on a sky only half full with clouds
saw a star falling and thought I could catch it
    I found I had too many useless dreams   understood
    why Dante iced Lucifer at the center of Hell

I lost a love I thought everlasting
if only betrayal were not concealed behind a mask of truth
if only there were a Martinella bell warning of the advance of evil
    I found myself standing like a lonesome tree at the edge
    of a cliff; I saw Polaris in the distance   I followed her.

The Dawn Wind

And the Wind dies down in the grass. It is day and his work
is done.

Rudyard Kipling   (1882-1956)

AT THAT TIME

At that time   when everything that is ends
    starts my journey to the land of forgotten ghosts
    if there were such a place for ghosts remembered or forgotten

At that time   it will be hard to untie the ties of love
    that sustained me. Would someone be
    at the other side of the moon   waiting?

At that time   I will be ready to stand by myself before the void
    since I learned to be in the company of aloneness
    I'll stand alone to feel the last wind touch me

At that time   as the seventh day of the seventh month finds
    the joined Vega and Altair stars separated by the Milky Way
    I will smile at the wish tree of Tanabata

At that time   when all my time is gathered in a faint echo
    I will still hear my inner storyteller whisper
    That it was all worth it.

ABOUT THE AUTHOR

Pina Pipino's poetry appeared in her chapbooks and in her previous collections *Whispers and Voices* and *The Scent of Time*, as well as in anthologies and literary journals, such as *Floricanto Si, Through a Child's Eyes, A Stone unturned, Open Footnote, Icon, Café Solo, Lips, Sensations Magazine, Shot Glass*, etc. She has been a finalist in poetry contests like *The Refined Savage Bilingual Review*, and received poetry prizes in the Allen Ginsberg's competitions as well as honorary mentions from the *Paterson Literary Review*.

Her short stories were published in *Forum Artium* and *Feminaria*. Her essays appeared in *Diario la Prensa of New Jersey*. She has written a novel currently with a NYC agent, and two novellas. She is preparing her fourth poetry collection.

Pipino has an MFA from Montclair State University. She finds poetry in the human expression, which she translates into sculptures and paintings that have been exhibited at City Without Walls and the Paterson Museum, in New Jersey, and at the Orange Gallery in New York. Her visual art is in permanent collections in Buenos Aires, New Jersey and Florida.

www.ingramcontent.com/pod-product-compliance
Lightning Source LLC
Chambersburg PA
CBHW020911090426
42736CB00008B/579

9 780578 207582